LETTERS TO TED

Some other books by Daniel Weissbort

Poetry
IN AN EMERGENCY
SOUNDINGS
LEASEHOLDER
FATHERS
INSCRIPTION
NIETZSCHE'S ATTACHÉ CASE
WHAT WAS ALL THE FUSS ABOUT?

Translation
NIKOLAY ZABOLOTSKY: SELECTED POEMS

As Editor
POST-WAR RUSSIAN POETRY
THE POETRY OF SURVIVAL

Criticism
FROM RUSSIAN WITH LOVE

Daniel Weissbort

Letters to Ted

Anvil Press Poetry

Published in 2002
by Anvil Press Poetry Ltd
Neptune House 70 Royal Hill London SE10 8RF
www.anvilpresspoetry.com

This book is published with financial assistance
from The Arts Council of England

Designed and set in Monotype Ehrhardt by Anvil
Printed and bound in England
by Cromwell Press, Trowbridge, Wiltshire

ISBN 0 85646 341 8

A catalogue record for this book
is available from the British Library

for V.P.

ACKNOWLEDGEMENTS

Some of these poems, some in earlier versions, appeared in: *Mississippi Review*, *Notre Dame Review*, *The Review*, *Iowa Review*, *The Poet's Voice*, *Acumen*, *Six Seasons Review* (India), *Passionate Renewal* (anthology), *European Judaism*, *Orbis*, *Magma* and *Chapman*.

AUTHOR'S NOTE

TED HUGHES, Poet Laureate, died on October 28, 1998. He and I had met in Cambridge in the mid '50s, when he was in his last year at Pembroke College, and I was beginning at Queens'. A small group of us would regularly gather in the Anchor pub, Silver Street, opposite Queens'.

Two magazines are mentioned in this collection. I played jazz piano at the party to launch the first of these, *Saint Botolph's Review*, which contained poems by Ted Hughes, David Ross (the editor), an American friend Lucas Myers, Daniel Huws and myself, as well as some other material. Only one issue of the magazine ever appeared (a second issue is being discussed at the time of writing). It was at this party that Ted Hughes met Sylvia Plath, an American Fulbright scholar, studying English at Newnham.

I wrote to Ted when he and Sylvia were in America and on their return to England began to see him again. Sylvia died in February 1963. At a New Year's party that year, Ted passed on to me an idea he had had in America for a magazine of modern poetry in English translation. I worked on this and the first issue of *Modern Poetry in Translation*, which we co-edited for a few issues, appeared in 1965. The early issues concentrated on work from Eastern Europe, such poets as Vasko Popa, János Pilinszky (on the translation of whose poetry Ted collaborated with a Hungarian friend and poet, János Csokits), Tadeusz Różewicz, Zbigniew Herbert and Miroslav Holub. I also "discovered" the Israeli poet Yehuda Amichai and brought his work to Ted. Ted translated Amichai's poetry, at first with his companion Assia Gutmann, later with the poet himself. In the year of Ted's death we collaborated on a translation of Pushkin's poem "The Prophet", and also on the selection of a volume of Yehuda Amichai's work in diverse translations. Both these tasks were completed shortly before Ted died and Faber published the Amichai selection in late 2000. The Pushkin translation, Ted's last poem, appeared in *After Pushkin* (Carcanet, 1999).

When Ted died, I was in America where until December 1999 I directed the Translation Workshop at the University of Iowa. I returned to England for a few days, travelling down to Devon, to North Tawton where the funeral service took place in St. Peter's Church. I also attended the memorial service in Westminster Abbey in May 1999.

In 1970 Ted had married Carol Orchard. With great kindness, after Ted's death, Carol invited me to Court Green on several occasions. A number of the pieces in the present collection were written during these visits. Others were written in Sewanee, Tennessee, in the home of Lucas Myers. The rest were written either in London, Iowa City or Keele, Staffordshire.

I had sent a large number of letters to Ted over the years, when I was mostly in America. On his death, I began writing what I am now calling "Letters to Ted", a sort of continuation of our correspondence – in recent years this had become rather one-sided in any case, although we continued to meet fairly regularly. I wrote these "letters" through 1999, attempting arbitrarily to bring them to a close at the turn of the century. Though there have been several more since, I have decided not to include them.

London
April, 2000

CONTENTS

Letters to Ted

GETTING THERE

I called from America. Frieda answered the phone.
I explained my predicament.

This morning I'm asking myself what she asked me:
What do you want to do?

We'd in common, Ted, wanting to please whoever had a
    claim . . .
but if one simply ignored them all?

Listening, eye on the road, concentrating on me or them,
you fitted together the fragments I presented you with . . .

"Disappoint", I'm muttering,
"not to be afraid to disappoint."

And you're nodding, wordlessly,
or just waiting for me to continue.

Tuesday morning
November 3, 1998

FLOWERS

I glanced into the room
where we'd sat only weeks before this,
reading Yehuda's poems in English,
sheets of paper piled on the floor,
or sliding over from the sofa.

An abundance, when there'd been
a mere half dozen, thirty years ago.

Today, the sofa was pushed back,
the floor strewn with bouquets instead.

STILL

Back in London,
why this pretence of talking or writing to you?
It is idle to address the dead,
even the recently dead,
even you, whom I've
pictured still hanging about,
as in Cambridge
fifty years ago.

DEPARTURE OF THE HEARSE

Noisy crows circle.
We stand in the rain.
We are waiting for the hearse to leave
with the body we've known you by.

INTRO

This week, in the British press,
the Great War –
the eightieth anniversary of its end.

That war was your intro, I suppose,
as mine was my Uncle Joe's account of Auschwitz.

You were my *England*.
Was I your *European Jewry*?

You brought back Eastern Europe from your travels,
and I stuck my foot in its door.

AMERICAS

I'm above the clouds,
over the Atlantic once more.
On my way back to America,
my penultimate return to
the land of opportunities!

We didn't share Americas,
though we might have done –
I'm making my way back.
And here at least, up here,
my America nods to yours.

Sunday
November 8, 1998

HYPERBOLE

You'd take me fishing with you –
I brought you luck, you said.
You'd scrutinize the bank for the right spot.
When I'd recaptured your attention,
I'd look for topics to reward you with.
Much or most you'd let pass.
Then I'd hit on something.
Your mind was more on the water,
but, as you noted where to cast,
your voice would come.

ALLY

Just as when we talked I'd feel
some deeper engagement had been foregone,
so even now I do not concentrate as I should.
I continue to summon words
which I'll return to later, to work over,
uncovering their spontaneity.

You seemed to approve of these tactics,
urging me to believe in them, myself,
snorting at the remarks of one editor, thirty years ago,
who said he was "a little uneasy" as to the music of my
    verse.

He put it well, I think,
but your indignation has stayed with me too,
your conviction that behind the provisionality, profligacy,
    sheer ineptitude,
lay some sort of truth-to-self.

You were my ally among the English!

"UNCLE WOLF"

I did not visit the wolves in Regent's Park Zoo.
Maybe next time I shall –
commiserate with the old wolf,
gaze upon his scragginess, his aloneness.

Then I'll sit in that pub, by Primrose Hill,
and remember them: "Dick, Jack, Dan . . .
And a curse on the age that loses the tune . . ."

I am midway through this 200-page notebook
and still there's been no taking up of words,
just a footing it from spot to spot,
holds dimly noted as I plod.

But I'll not put words in your mouth.
I know enough to know that all that matters now
is the will or courage to pursue an onwardness.

However halt or even compromised,
provisional it's not.

Life takes up the slack.

November 12, 1998

WINTER IS COMING IN

And winter is coming in.
The crows raised a ruckus as we left the church,
and there was a remark passed and some laughter,
and I nodded –
I suppose most of us did, at the appropriateness.
And now winter is coming in.

And at this moment I am almost happy,
in a bleakness not of your making,
or rather not of your death's making;
and also not happy to find
what I turn to as I think of you,
now one among others, so soon as well.

And winter, coming in, hesitates.
Winter, the winter you also anticipated,
except that an unbreachable barrier was thrown up.

And now, at this time,
which seems like a waiting time,
I consider the same winter,
staring across it
at what I do not recognize,
because you are not standing there.

And winter, sober, spare, is coming.
I hope at least to draw nourishment from
the passing above us of storms.

Saturday
November 14, 1998

YOUR DEATH?

What's happened to your death?
Have I lamented too much?
Already it is beginning to look *historical* –
with a date attached.

Cremation helped, the spirit freed,
as against the remembered majesty
of your bulk beside me in the car
between Court Green and Exeter.

But still I also see you brought up short,
see you gesture to no avail –
O, the unuttered, unheard words! –
and even the gesture, whisked away.

SILENTLY

We bumped along lanes,
scrambled over stiles,
down to a river we strolled by,
with you taking stock –

then through a meadow,
climbing a hill,
across some more fields,
back to the road by another route,

and the car again.
Then, bumping up the steep track,
and home to Court Green
by moonlight.

There was a quality of silence
in your meanderings, me by your side,
makes me now think of János Pilinszky . . .
who wanted to write poems "as if I had remained silent".

OUR MAGAZINE

You stood there,
a stillness about you.
On your own, then, in a corner of Kim's flat.
It was New Year's Eve, 1963–4.

You told me your idea for a magazine –
explaining quite systematically, I imagine,
unprompted and yet somehow as if you had been.

It was a simple enough idea, if original,
modern poetry in translation, just that.
"At least a novelty", the *TLS* called it.

WHAT'S LEFT

It is pre–dawn and I am awake.
You are still dead,
even if your last words to me
seem so much a part of life
that I'm puzzled.

But I scold myself . . .
Who am I to *puzzle*!
This is not *proper*.
Already I've exceeded the bounds
of proper regret or sorrow.

I turn to you – has anything changed? –
and each time rejoice,
finding you unchanged.

After the farm was sold,
your pet pedigree bull, Sexton Hyades the 33rd,
was exhumed and his bones brought to Court Green
for reburial in your garden.
You'd wanted to see what was left of the bull.

A taurean bust was to be placed over the burial mound.

And so it was. After your death,
a shockingly lifelike effigy, it presides,
a veritable minotaur head.

Tuesday
16 November, 1998
pre–dawn

NARRATIVE

to Yehuda Amichai

Narratives were appealing, Freud, Jung and so forth.
You did not aggrandize or heroicize,
least of all yourself.

I watched the narratives being assembled,
in particular what got told towards the end,
the Ovid especially.

You stood behind the song, the narrative, wherever.
For instance, in Yehuda's re-telling in English
what he had told first in his own tongue.

REMEMBER CAMBRIDGE!

Your rendering of Sir Patrick Spens.
I recall the song, of course. And your voice, almost.
But, in any case, the voice ceased –
later I tried to remember when that was, and why.

As for our qualms about Sylvia,
it seems, you never forgot,
I don't know that you forgave either –
your memory let none of it go.

And so you kept current
what the rest would rather have or had let go.
You allowed it to be judged again,
or perhaps for the first time.

That you could not or would not forget
renders ordinarily human
what was mythologized by strangers.

THE COMPLETE WORKS

The gnarled power of your start –
we had to make do with echoes, however strong.
It was as if, whether you or we liked it or not,
the times decreed otherwise –

as they did for your Shakespeare.
When I admitted once I'd not read Timon of Athens –
or perhaps it was Pericles –
you stared in mock (maybe real?) amazement,

followed by some gruff comment.
It was somehow gratifying to concur with this reproach.
But while I turned quite often to the Complete Works,
the project remained – as it remains still – unrealized.

Wednesday
November 17, 1998

NO ALIAS

Hard to believe you've not left an alias in your place,
or that it's not an alias died instead of you.
Too final for one who endlessly surprised us with his
        metamorphoses,
his resurrections or reincarnations, as Brodsky called them.

I wait, we wait, knowing though
that now there will be no resurrection.
It seems *contre nature*,
but that's just the point –
it *is* natural, *with* nature not against.

It is natural now for you to be wordless
who were one of the great prestigiators,

a ventriloquist of the first order,
giving nature voice.

Of course, one didn't quite believe one's ears.
But that only put us on your side, the maker's.
What was understood bound us to you,
as we waited for your next improvisation.

PLAYING THE GAME

I think at first you tried to ignore it.
Then, perhaps, as was your custom,
you tried to make something of it,
to capture its attention,
to engage it in conversation.

Meanwhile the rest of us started to worry,
confronted by its inexorableness.
Still, though the process was clearly under way,
in company you continued to ignore it,
not letting it run the show,
even as it took hold.

So far you'd still your strength,
were still in charge.
You managed yourself,
brought yourself to the place of drastic remedies;
in company you were not melancholic,
even if a loosening of the connections troubled you now.

The will, that is, continued to resist.
You yourself would not give in –
it became a kind of game,
an end-game.

And here, too, it's a game!
I pretend that the outcome may be changed,
the body rally in good time,
the rebellion be put down,
the scattered senses come to their senses,
the refusal to submit receive its due reward,
your destiny be returned to you and to us

Wednesday–Thursday
November 18, 1998

GORDIAN KNOT

It may be true that you didn't cut Gordian knots.
Yet, in the end, some of those who loved you didn't expect
     you to.
It was not weakness, I think,
not indecisiveness, irresponsibility,
as others thought.

Of course, there's a psychological side to this –
youngest child, conciliator, reasoner.
And certainly you reasoned,
as did I, also the younger child.

Sometimes you and I even reasoned together,
with multiplying arguments,
rather than excuses.

It was a game, not unlike writing poems –
at least for me it was.
But you always went one better,
following your own trajectory, uninfluenced by mine.
Your flights of fancy were monologues,
each with its individual propulsion . . .

But what of those Gordian knots?

I think you strove for seamlessness,
for continuity, intensity,
for improvisation –
if one *can* strive for improvisation –
at worst for patching up.
Though *was* it worst?
Your life was the narrative.

There were no Gordian knots to cut,
not from the point of view of narrative,
or individual lives.

MNEMONICS

In my absence doors closed, people died.
This time, I move slowly towards the door –
eventually I'll close it,
surrendering the key to my successor.
Once outside, will I gaze at the sky
and offer up a prayer?
Or will emptiness assail me?

You'd have shown interest in such a situation.
Places, filled or vacated by us,
as we arrive, depart,
as we dispose of what's left of a life –
you'd lots to say about that sort of thing.

So, I am tidying up behind me,
but it's questionable whether or not I shall continue.
Perhaps I'll manage one more cross-over
between back there and what might succeed it.
Perhaps I'll just peter out,
having completed the last chores.
Or quite likely what's marked out for me
is simply the beginning of a new phase –
broadly speaking, the consequence of survival!

Again I marvel at your endurance,
the blows that scuppered you,
as they were bound to, your resurrections,
and the effort needed to connect all this,
to keep the lines open.

Such endurance, courage, refusal to submit –
of course, the strain told.
The silences testified to those separations.
And your approach to memory, through narrative,
connecting things with no logical connection,
so your lives could remain apart but linkable,
the machinery in good working order.

The games you tried as well to teach
compensated for the limits placed on talk –
though you talked more and more,
increasingly voicing the hitherto unvoicable,
as if you were speaking to yourself –
or so it seemed, it was so unprecedented.

It was like a cry, yet without expectation of an answer,
though one longed to offer help.
Instead, one shared observations with you,
acknowledging perhaps that the message had been
      received.
And who is to say that's not as much as you allowed
      yourself to hope for?

Saturday
November 21, 1998

ART CONFUSED

Back then, insofar as we discussed literature,
it was, among other things, to excoriate free verse
and, I dare say, first-person poetry too.
This, we thought, was self-indulgent;
impersonality was the goal;
the White Goddess's magisterial eye, rather than Eliot's,
    kept us under perpetual judgment.

So, does art give up the ghost when truth to self's at
    stake?
Finally, art and a kind of ignorance or innocence should be
    evenly matched.
You seemed to think that, in this respect,
your own prodigious talent was no advantage,
but an obstacle perhaps.

Thursday
November 26, 1998
Thanksgiving

31

TRANSLATION

The plays you translated you made something of,
your translations of the verse of friends comparatively
    little –
as though this had been dictated.
But how clearly you had heard,
how vividly, vigorously did you transcribe!
As for your "X-ray vision" . . .
You were attacked on account of it, for being too literal,
in that you told no more than you saw or heard,
keeping your eye on the task, not yourself.
Still, the words *were* yours.
But if you knew this – how could you not have known! –
evidently it did not trouble you,
as it might have me, for instance.
On the contrary, you accepted the odds,
accepted the dilemma, which was a human one,
and unabashedly lent the writing your strength and skill.
I was convinced that each time you gave yourself,
you were responding to a kind of call to learn.
Maybe what you learnt was just to give.
The voices of your peers had also to be heard and loved –
that's what it was to be of their company.
But you had to serve yourself –
just as you yourself had to serve,
and it was yourself as well you'd to deliver every time.

CLUTTER

The emptying of the house reminds me that
you said you liked clutter.

You talked of weeds, flowering, fruiting.
But I suppose people, as they will, tidied up about you,
even though you yourself had an instinct for order.

Still, "Don't throw anything out!" you growled.
"Put it all in boxes", you commanded.
I tried and, as far as I was able to, did.

But gradually I burrowed into these too, disposed of
    fistfuls.
"To keep things manageable", I persuaded myself.
That is, I dealt with the situation in an ad-hoc manner,
But as if there were some method to it.

I'm reminded of this, as I box what remains unboxed.
It's slim pickings.

Sunday
November 29, 1998

FENG SHUI

The unnatural warmth is supposed to end today,
more seasonal weather, they say, will return.
At last my house looks empty –
maybe *tranquil* is the word?

It's almost as though this tranquillity,
long, long in the making,
had always existed.

Yesterday, I recounted, how last summer,
you gave me a book on Feng Shui,
and, with characteristic hyperbole, growled:
It'll change your life!

I tried it once,
tirelessly bringing objects together with their selves –
"Lovely, lovely", murmured my visitor.

As you see, I censored her name –
Who knows why! What bothers me more
is how I spoke of you –
in tranquillity, as if you were part of the arrangement.

Sunday
December 5, 1998

SLEIGHT OF HAND

We're just waiting for you to find your way back,
with a half laugh, to address us,
the long head, heavy,
familiarly squared shoulders,
the eyes, levelling.

But the quiet's a dead give-away.

February 16, 1999

HEAR

Jorge Luis Borges visited Iowa City.
Seated on stage, the blind man spoke into a dead mike
while we all pretended we could hear.

Even as I write this, you're hard at it –
it seems not to matter to you
or you don't know you cannot be heard.

Though maybe you can.
Maybe, if I really tried . . .

You were just telling me.

Monday, March 1, 1999

COURT GREEN AFTER

We've been talking –
perhaps the more freely, because
you can surely listen in.
Not like someone who's had a stroke
and is simply parked in the flow of talk.

We must be patient.
A sort of expectancy informs our conversation,
As if your presence were about to manifest itself.
But how long, I ask, how long?

Everywhere there are signs –
Objects waiting to be picked up
or passed over by you.
They lapse into a state that should be temporary,
but is becoming permanent.

Here are your glasses, in an open case,
the cord wound round the bridge,
chunky, a big man's glasses,
old age still a puzzle.

Here's a letter to your Dutch translator,
painstaking answers and a command:
Don't print these,
I may use them myself somewhere, some time.
You did not have death in mind.

And the photo, 1954,
Pembroke College graduates,
the man at the end of the second row
gazing, smooth-cheeked,
twenty-four year old beau . . .

Grey skies, rain all day.
The cobbled yard –
as if you were outside my bedroom door.
Too big for the corridor,
stooped, head bowed.

You turn away, floorboards creak.
Head lifted now, close to the ceiling.
Carrying them away,
the long-lipped smile,
the dead-reckoning eye.

LITERALNESS

I still lack a measure for you,
keep returning to the literalness.

Too much for many. For me as well?
Still, work with translation gave me a clue.

In any case, the experience of literalness
took me to where you were.

Now I approach you again, or try –
in the solemn-serious spirit of non-reverence,
which is also a kind of literalness.

PEDAGOGUE

"A Bedtime Story. Where you can't walk take a leap."
You wrote these words in my copy of the magnum opus.
So substantial a tome, wasn't this rather disingenuous?

Now, with relief, it occurs to me
that you meant exactly what you said:
"A bedtime story."

Of course, behind the injunction to "take a leap"
was another, more familiar one:
Read it all!

Still, why did it have to be your death
made me take you at your word,
to leap about in your garden of visionary things?

A DEDICATION

The Zabolotsky volume arrived on Friday.
I'd coupled your name to Brodsky's.
But now all thoughts of others, of Joseph even,
were driven from my head.

I manoeuvred between your two mentoring voices.
And now I've chained them together in my dedication.
How uneasily these two names occupy the same page.

And as for him, the man himself,
he'd have managed without either of you,
and certainly he didn't need both,
as doubtless you'd have been the first, simultancously,
    to acknowledge.

Saturday–Sunday.
March 7–8, 1999
3.30 a.m

SOME THOUGHTS ON THE THOUGHT-FOX

for Valentina

I was urged to remember poems.
I did remember fragments
of poems I'd once known in their entirety.

Waking at three a.m, I'd still in mind
the anthology I might assemble:
Charge of the Light Brigade,
speeches from Henry Five,
Auden on Yeats, Heaney on Brodsky etc.
Then there was another sequence
starting with Dylan Thomas, Poem in October . . .

And finally another one
beginning with your Thought-Fox,
so often commented on by you,
sacrificed over and over on the altar of readings.
And in that context, my own "thought-fox" poem, as it
    were,
also set in Cambridge. I wrote about
a moth that came to my door, or rather window,
"spawn of the black, impressive night . . ."
No thought process there,
a mere fleck on the lens of my sleeplessness.

I picture your Thought-Fox,
like the Netsuke image on the cover of *Wolfwatching*.
You inscribed that book: "At least
the creature on the cover is appealing, with its hopeful tail".
The chunky little wolf's front paws are raised,
as it casts a sidelong, wicked glance at us.

At least, what the Fox told was plain enough.
Perhaps it was too plain, too obvious?
In the end, you did not heed its warning,
though what choice had you?
Still you'd recited this verse often enough.
Couldn't we have applauded your original intention to
    comply?

ANOTHER DEDICATION

You wrote in my copy of *Birthday Letters*: "Before us stands
    yesterday."
When I saw the film-tribute, "Ted Hughes, Force of
    Nature",
I was taken aback to hear your old school chum read the same
    dedication, word for word, in *his* copy of the book –
I'd taken "*us*" to be a reference to you and me.

But in any case, surely you didn't mean there was no way
    forward,
that henceforth there'd be time only for summaries?
That sounds more like me than you,
uncharacteristically defeatist, unless . . . Well,
unless you were simply describing *Birthday Letters*?

So, I didn't agree.
I resisted the fatalism, as I took it to be.
Although, at the same time, I did agree that mostly what lay
    ahead was a re-working of the past.
Still, I was surprised, disappointed that you'd put it so
    bluntly.

Your old school chum simply said:
"Marvellous, isn't it!"

BLACK ICE

You'd stopped to pick up some flies from a shop,
exiting, leapt onto a low wall that was coated with black ice.

I should have known about such things from Iowa,
yet as you plunged your full great length,
springing to your aid, I skidded neatly, bloodying myself
    as well.

When I think now of that double act of ours,
it's the sudden materiality I recall –
you plummeted into your self and rose, yourself again,
as if you'd not been till that moment.

HAVING ONE'S SAY

No, I've not had my say,
but life's had it for me.
Life reared back and shouted me down.
And for as long as I didn't hang on to your coat-tails,
I've been looking the other way,
Aware or thinking that you were there.

And even now, as I blather,
at least half an ear on the critics,
who correctly point out the obvious
or don't even need to,
I dare not eye the inner dark
where your likeness vanishes
and the actual you again takes over.

Well, *dare not* isn't quite right either.
Do not. I wait for you to insist,
to crack open the door with yourself standing there.
And naturally I do gather something,
scraps of what you left behind,
nothing current.

These scraps are all I have to go by.
I do not ask myself what you're saying –
after all, what *would* you be saying to me now?
There are too many imponderable questions.
Though I no longer believe I can come up with the goods,
what have I got to lose!
And if it's so much fantasy,
at least there's something to be learnt:
the one life we have is not to be kept under wraps until
    all's known.

Life is to be lived, in ignorance and error,
whether dressed up in resplendent language,
or gaped at in its nakedness.

And that brings me back to you,
who strove mightily for meaning,
looking for larger systems, narratives.
And you kept telling these,
with modifications, variations –
but the same too.

Perhaps this eased the pain?

You took my hapless words
and connected them to some tale or other.
A distant look would come into your eye –
a storyteller's look,
this was what conversation was for me as well,
the two of us, simultaneously narrating –
from whatever starting point,
trying also to identify what and where that point was,
in whatever larger scheme.

The feeling that one should be about one's business
has always existed.
And now the realization comes
that, inevitably perhaps, the job might not get done.

A BAD MISTAKE

You were badly mistaken,
as you acknowledged in the end,
able to do so only when it was too late.
You cleared the ground for a final push,
when there was no ground left,
only an edge to tumble over.

But then the scale was commensurate with you!
We knew, you knew.
And yet it was still as if you had been picked,
while the rest of us took a few knocks,
but generally kept our heads down.

For the time being we've taken our knocks.
But you have been parted from your words.

Sunday
March 21st, 1999

TAKING YOU WITH ME

The writer is one who'll not settle for silence!
I remember – Henry Miller, it was –
a reference to the sage Vivekananda's contention
that the names of the true prophets were unknown,
that for every Christ-publicist, there was a silent seer.

Were the spoken words the Christ's true cross?
Did he sacrifice his silence?

And you, too? Reticence, yes, but did it come naturally?
In the end, you had a go.
You wandered about, accustoming people to yourself and
    yourself to them.
And part of you stayed behind, preparing the last phase.

That's what inevitably I bring with me on my travels:
leftover silence, what was not accomplished,
literally beyond you who had prepared the ground so
    meticulously.

Tuesday
March 28th, 1999

YOUR VOICE INSIDE THE ABBEY

Unannounced, your voice filled the Abbey,
startling us, keeping us startled.
Suddenly it wasn't the words –
that song from Cymbeline,
wonderful words though they be –
but life itself wanting you to live.
Your voice, unaccompanied by you,
the senses wouldn't accept just voice.
Anger at your non-appearance –
resignation forced on us –
there in the Abbey of English Kings,
in the presence of a diminutive queen and a solicitous,
    frowning prince.
The nails of the knowledge of your death were hammered in
with every utterance,
as we were sung to, seduced.

OUR JOB

Now you're the talk of our town too.
No more kidding – we've succumbed
to your success, your grandest failure.
And we carry on.
We joke, laugh, chatter.
We're not keeping you alive.
In the absence of witnesses
who might make a difference,
it seems we've a job to do.

IN GREYS

I see you in greys, untowering,
in the middle distance,
approaching, unapproachable,

in your thirties or forties.
respectful, unbohemian, uncertain –
evidently, though not really.

I see you as an ordinary bloke,
embarrassed, too much talent,
pockets with gifts, with toys.

You remain in that middle distance.
I see you, but cannot convey it,
unlike you, who got it down on paper.

You're all of a piece, too human, too ordinary.
You endured manfully,
you endured helplessly,

as far as I can tell,
unquestioningly,
accepting your destiny.

You accepted the odds,
as you once wrote of those others,
of Vasko, Zbigniew, Miroslav, János.

And what did they make of you,
from beyond the vortex,
beset by your own catastrophe?

Is it this, though, that has barged you back for me
into some peak manhood? Now
I see you approaching again, approachable.

Karlovy Vary
June 18, 1999

BAND STAND: KARLOVY VARY

Since you've left all this behind now,
it's a little hard to explain.
But I live on, for a while at least.
So, though I'd like to ignore what's happened,
it wouldn't be right.
And to pretend I'm talking it over with you
is just as unacceptable really.
Because the fact is, I'm *not* talking it over with you.
All I *can* do is recall what we once discussed,
recovering what I understood at the time,
and now perhaps a little more besides.
There's probably a time limit on such ruminations.
But we're still distractedly searching the ruins.
Eventually, in the not so distant or radiant future,
my own little brass band will strike up again.
It's already had several practice runs.

June 18, 1999

EEL-FISHING

for Peter Norton-Smith

It was dark, as during the blitz.
We tramped down to the river to fish for eels.
A high bank. A shed to warm ourselves in.

A fire, a pan . . .
You lent me a rod.
I hung it into the blackness,
a smudge or glitter here and there.
And then a pull. I announced this.

Tug! I did.
Total resistance.

Tug! I did, as embarrassed
as whatever had darted under something below was deep,
although it was maybe shallow.

At any rate, it was more than a match for me.
I tugged and was free!
What? Laughter.

"He's broken the best eel rod,
supposed to be unbreakable . . ."
Laughter. Apologies from me.
More laughter.

At your funeral, Peter remarked:
"Do you remember the eel-fishing?"
"Of course . . ." I laughed.

LETTERS FROM ICELAND

I like it here, barely peopled,
all verticals and horizontals —
and a shadowless twilight.

And a different ocean.

You'd have homed in on this land.
Not like Auden & MacNeice.
You'd have internalized the combustion!

All I can do is write again to you,
except that already I've moved on a bit,
whereas you are stuck in the rut of your death.

You came to fish in virgin waters
but Japanese businessmen got there before.
You never told me of your disappointment,
but you called Iceland "a gigantic cinder".

That's hardly fair!

This land is not burnt out, but hyper-active.
Perhaps impatience supervened?
Still, surely the thermal abundance pleased?
Contemplating the rushing steam,
quaffing the sulphuric air . . .

Ash underfoot, steam.
Twice, in close succession,
Geyser's little brother greeted us,
myself and Valentina.

The coffee machine burbles and sighs.
A stretch of unpeopled time,
so the mind's people, whoever,
may assemble centre stage,
whatever and wherever . . .

I think we shared some such dream
there's maybe a whiff of in the air here.

July 11, 1999

UNTRANSLATED

Do I preserve what I know by not transcribing you,
not finding a form of words for you –
the look of you and your way of looking?
Do I keep you in the original,
untranslated?

August 20, 1999

CORNUCOPIA

Last night, in Devon, abundance,
lobsters and a cornucopia of berries.

I'm put in mind of that photograph
of you with my small son Benjamin, at a wedding.
You are hovering above Ben, smiling goofily.
Ben, his head cocked, looks up at the camera.
The table is laden with fruits.

Already it's next morning.
I'm lying in bed, in the quiet, waiting for what?
Downstairs, the Sunday papers
and the certainty you are not there.

Sunday morning
August 22, 1999

PITY THE MAN WHOM ALL MEN LOVE

At each move, a new outcry.
Even now, after your death,
your appearances tend to provoke this.

The scholars band together,
fortifying the narrow view,
leaking an order to die of unfulfilment in.

I hear a murmurous laughter?
Your eyes lower, your lips curl.
A string of curses follows.

"Pity the man", you muttered once,
when I tried to commiserate with you,
"whom all men love".

HEALER

It was not so long after my cancer surgery,
you took me to the healer, Ted Cornish,
who once had cured *your* back.

He sat me in a chair and stood behind it.
You stood behind him.
Cornish talked of this and that –
it was better if I didn't think too hard,
better for him, too, not to concentrate.
Only, he asked me if I felt a warmth.

I did, and a tingling –
and that was all there was to it.
Except for some chat between Cornish and yourself.
And perhaps, as was your custom on any visit,
you regaled us with a tale or two,
and Cornish, I am sure, kept his end up,
as befitted so renowned a healer.

Now, when I think of it, I say to myself:
"Yes, I remember Ted Cornish."
And then I wonder what became of him.

The last I heard was that he had retired.
At the time, I thought: how odd for a healer to retire.
But why not? Healing's a job like any other.

NOT SAINT BOTOLPH'S: AN ANTIDOTE

How much do I remember?
A party, New Year's Eve, 1963–4,
Sylvia almost a year dead.
How much did I know?

You were on your own.
I probably talked and talked,
and, for whatever reason,
you came out with the idea you'd had
for a magazine of poetry-in-translation . . .

Thirty-six years have passed
but the magazine remained your protégé.
It joined us in an enterprise
that maybe got you going again –
after Sylvia.

A kind of antidote,
not Saint Botolph's.

BETRAYAL?

To return to the dream of two nights ago . . .

How did I betray you?
How did it come about that I was the betrayer?

After all, I've dreamed it more than once . . .

What confidences had I taken advantage of,
used to *my* advantage?

       . . .

"A Kurdish practice", Kevin said.
"I want to try this out on you."

I lay on the floor,
and he bent, twisted, pulled my limbs about,
arranging them neatly in the end.
Then he trod on my soft tissues,
the hands especially,
pressing the whole of me into the floor.

After that he left me for an age.

I diverted myself in several ways, including the following:
"Where are you, Ted?" I asked.
I seemed weightless,
the body adamantly floored
or *grounded*, as Kevin had put it,
not thinking directly of the question I'd just formulated,
but somehow holding that single thought in mind.

And you hovered a little.

All my own weight, as I think I said,
was in my limbs. The self
had sunk down, bodily, beyond,
and rested there now,
at some ultimate point, a lookout,
from which, I looked out upon you,
selecting you from among several possibilities.

Later, I speculated that
for me, perhaps, betrayal signified
what my writing struggled with
and tried to but could not overcome.
Perhaps it was this allowed me to make use
of what you'd given me,
or what I'd helped myself to,
or what just somehow came my way.

Certainly, betrayal it was,
as all writing maybe is.

Perhaps.

There's no *perhaps* about it!

Still, I may have let myself off too easily,
literally making light of you –
so that I did not feel the weight.

Caught out two nights ago,
I quailed before you and your accusations,
until inertia set in.

By then, though, you'd stalked off,
even if I tried to bring you back,
to float you once more in my sky.

September 21, 1999
a.m.

ON YOUR RETINUE

You'd this retinue
that sometimes, despite your own reverberations,
all but shouted you down.

Even now, my memory of you is accompanied by a babble.
Yet such, I suppose, was your gravity,
that still you came, dragging them behind,
almost as if unaccompanied. Indeed,
you made quite a show of being unaccompanied,
and one humoured you, because what else could one do,
wishing for you the singleness, aloneness
that you maybe wished for yourself.

But you also loved to entertain – I'd almost forgotten that –
culinary marvels you introduced to others, myself for one,
by so much exceeding any earlier self-indulgence!

The retinue, however, was not of such.
Rather was it a wakened world,

woken, that is, by your electricity,
the dent you made, pulling into orbit the local gods and
  goddesses.

It was not that you were unaware of this,
this company or accompaniment,
but that deliberately you did not draw attention to it,
as if it was protected by your aura.
If you did not allude to it,
if the effort was unseen by others,
you could preserve, protect for a while
the threatened angelic orders.

VENICE AND THE RICE DIET

I announced I was going to Venice. You interjected:
"Let me know if the canals really stink!"
and then marched me into Daunt's and made me buy
Jan Morris's book on Venice: "The best on any city."

Even if I myself had not been to Venice,
it surprised me – why should it have done? –
that you had never been there.
I was shocked by your lack of reverence.

But as we walked along Marylebone High Street,
me holding the book you'd made me purchase,
the air was as good as London air can be
and I recounted what I had put by for you.

I told you of the diet of rice,
brought to the boil and drained three times;
thus deglutinated, when slowly chewed,
it absorbed impurities like a sponge.

Now I am mortified by my own insensitivity,
my ill-rehearsed babble about thrice-boiled rice,
when, for you, as it turned out
the end was in sight already.

I see you walking very slowly, head bowed,
nodding, as though to give what I'd been saying,
the gravest consideration, compensating maybe
for the earlier slight, your irreverence.

Just as well I stopped, letting you depart.
You hailed a cab, climbed in. Before this,
with that blunt yet old-world courtesy of yours,
you offered to drop me off somewhere.

A TRANSLATION

You took that poem by Juhasz Ferenc,
"The Boy Changed into a Stag Cries out at the Gate of
    Secrets", in the McRobbie version,
and carried it with you into the upper reaches of Court
    Green,
and some hours later reappeared with it, rewritten, typed
    out on your old portable –
this was for the Hungarian issue of our journal.

The issue was never published.
But I kept your translation, for a long time,
together with other Hungarian translations by you,
the latter, though, modelled on your friend János Csokits's
　　rigorous literals.

"The Boy" was different.
Here, what you saw in that other version
somehow pressed so urgently on you
that you'd only to get it down.

So, what became of it?

Eventually, I returned the manuscript to you,
since the issue never came out.
I didn't see it again.
And when, many years later, I asked,
having in view once more a Hungarian issue
and hoping to link it to our earlier attempt,
you said you didn't know what had become of it.

So vividly did I recall the translation,
not the words but that trek of yours upstairs and re-
　　emergence with a complete alternative text,
that your vagueness as to its whereabouts surprised me.

But now I wonder.
Could it be, you didn't want to look again
at what was all in the doing?

Or, perhaps it is not lost at all,
but lying in your archives, where it should remain,
as illegitimate and innocent as on the day of its making.

LUCKY!

I don't remember the actual moments
you heaved fish into the air
and dispatched them, when fetched thither,
with a blow to the brow,
their lengths, at length, at peace.

They were to be taken to friends,
Sean and his wife, for instance –
their diminutive cottage,
your head close to the beams,
simply too much for that interior!

But those moments, no memory of them,
or perhaps, if I concentrate?

You often caught something when I was there –
you said I brought you luck –
but to me it seemed the fish came of their own accord,
so you'd not leave empty-handed.

And even if I do not recall the actual times,
I do recall the Dart's other bank,
perpendicular, inaccessibly dense.
Your line slithered across to that side.
The transparent surface was something tangible I grew
    aware of,
staring through to the mottled floor.
Fish were grey-brown shapes, motionless –
until the telltale swirl or flick.

You stared, observed, and cast, cast,
drawing your fly across, over those silhouettes.

That they'd have to seize it –
even if I don't like to say so –
was part of an order of things.

Evening
Friday, 24 September

SAINT BOTOLPH'S REVIEW

Came across a small stock.
The magazine, spare,
with a flawlessness owned from the start,
had survived, impervious to aging.

Would I recognize myself now –
that red-nosed piano player?
No memory of the others –
none of Sylvia, not even you,

for instance, that you'd predicted disaster
(a "planetary certainty"). After all
you'd not infrequently cried wolf,
knowing that no one, yourself included, would pay
      attention.

But it was you brought me along!
I'd caught cold and was determined to stay home, in
      Queens'.
You called on me, administered a potion . . .

So, what's left?
Rosencrantz and Guildenstern,
an I-was-there part.
I think I remember that small piece of the story –

your irresistible counter-claim,
myself raised from my bed of safety,
inducted into life-and-death,
my first taste of it maybe,

death right there, in our midst, one of us,
though it's you were spotlit,
you the light clung to,
as in a movie.

The noise might have died away –
Lyde and his band, myself on piano –
leaving just you and she,
in slow motion,
you, your eye adrift,
she, wholly fixed on you,
with that uncertain smile.

The magazine,
half a century on,
seems not to have aged a day.

THE GARDEN

You built yourself a hut in the garden, on a rise –
or was it your father built it? –
which for a while you shared with hornets,
so you could "rid the house of my idle presence".

It seemed to me – in my ignorance, it's true –
you never got that garden right.
Apparently, you disliked the extent of lawn,
planting a line of dwarf trees, to contour and divide its
        sweep.

But why did you countenance it for so long?
Were you just complying with the notion of an English
        country garden: tea on the lawn etcetera?
Still, such immaculateness did seem alien –
perhaps that was true of Devon as a whole.
You told me once, too, that Devon sent you to sleep.
But you stayed. Perhaps sleep is what you needed.

So, though you fiddled with it, you accepted the garden on
        its own terms,
and only latterly did you aspire to impose your own,
as you did on your whole environment and oeuvre.
Was it because you knew it was too late?

Now you are gone and a bull's head presides,
on its own mound, just down from that hut –
one large question-mark in this green and Christian land.
There is something artless, provisional about it,
from a draft, maybe, of a larger project?

DEVON TO WALES

Last night, roused from a dream of journeying,
I remembered your forcefulness:
"Let's go!"

We got into the car,
drove from Devon to Wales,
to be with our bereaved friend and his wife.

A daughter's sudden death. We sat with them,
in the familiar kitchen,
you awkwardly jammed into the corner.

And for a while,
everything was back in place,
as if it was always a possibility.

Back to this or to that,
back, for instance,
to the joyful birth of a daughter.

September 29, 1999
5.00 a.m.

HARTLAND

I went there several times
but only once or twice with you.
I remember the view, of course,
the world writ large.
But better than that,
our lounging on the shingle beach below,
you casting stones into the ocean.

But what we talked of,
your actual words, or mine,
all of that is gone.
Only your attitude, thoughtful,
with you propped on an elbow,
eyes narrowed in the wind –
you're nibbling something,
a blade of grass,
you're lobbing stones.

A tiny, battleship-grey cove,
the waters unagitated –
air with gulls –
a few clouds, not a sunny day.

Not as if we had descended from up there,
but as though we'd dropped out of sight,
were playing truant,
idling on a beach of stones.

ORDINARY

Not genius but being ordinary
ought to have protected you.
You didn't make a spectacle of yourself,
but kept your head down.

Even now, a year on,
I expect to be told that it was an error,
the drama concerned somebody else,
a case of mistaken identity.

But then, even in *my* foolish imagining,
the brute facts stare back:
you were walloped into submission,
your resistance was brushed aside.

You were reduced and then disposed of.
All that remains is the trail, the scent.
Ordinary? What's so ordinary?
Still, it is. As if you just walked off.

THE CURE

All your life, you looked for a cure.
Shakespeare was maybe it.
But in writing that book, you did yourself in –
at least that's what you suspected.
Ironical!

I think you got close to a cure.
Over the short run,
you kept rediscovering it,
the poem sequences hanging in
like grim death.

MY CURIOSITY

For a year I've been interrogating you.
Sometimes I have indeed put words into your mouth.
But I see now that you've vouchsafed nothing.

You seem to me to have been left behind,
stripped and abandoned by death.
It's as if you were waiting for it to return and collect you.

In such circumstances,
How can you be expected to answer my questions,
to indulge my curiosity!

WAS IT NATURE?

I listen to your voice –
so quiet and persuasive.
But who is it persuading now?

How many words through clenched teeth,
as if you were talking to yourself,
or rehearsing.

You threw a series of trick balls.
They came out of nowhere or your genius,
not really yours, as if you'd disowned it.

But you performed your poems lovingly,
even if not owning them, even
as if no particular credit were due, or just a little.

You melted into nature,
as your otter into water.
But was it nature, or Chaucer, Shakespeare?

I insist that you invented a version of nature,
gave it your colours, your sense of the sacred.
In short, that it was also the real thing.

Through clenched teeth,
you answer: "Maybe!"
Maybe, Maybe, Maybe!

A HYPOTHESIS

Was it that the prose did you in,
as your Thought-Fox had warned?
You read that poem over and over,
recited it, recorded it, told it,
yet in the end ignored the warning.

I expect you owed it to the Bard.
If *it* hadn't done you in, wouldn't *he* have?
Anyway, surely the prose, as such, wasn't responsible.

What did you in, perhaps, was the waxing of your powers.
Translation's muse beckoned, hugged you.
Only she turned out to have more limbs than Siva.

Ovid, OK. But then there was Aeschylus, Euripides,
the *Gawain* poet, *Gilgamesh*, on and on probably.
They stepped almost simultaneously from the wings,
into a corridor that dwindled away.

And so you set out,
even knowing you'd have to dispose of them at some point.
At some point, you'd have to turn,
to attend to other business, your own.
Perhaps you hadn't the heart.

Wednesday
November 18, 1999
4 a.m.

OUR CAMBRIDGE

What of Cambridge, Cambridge itself?
We spoke of it only to malign or mock it.

Or it was the unspoken –
we'd got there, after all, we'd *arrived* –
from our various points of origin –
it was our destination, for now.

That is, for then!
Cambridge lifted itself also above and around us,
like a keep, a labyrinth.
It was an indecipherable stage in our lives.

Hence the alternative Cambridge we cobbled together –
out of a refusal to join in.
But how much this took its cue from the real thing
is also indecipherable.
It seems to have mimicked the latter.

I'd like to think Cambridge was surprised by us.
We entered at an odd angle, or so I'd like to think.
Still, what happened was that we glanced off it,
insofar as we were noticed at all, were successfully repelled.
Cambridge was like a magnet, pushing us away.
But pushing back, we lingered a little,
pressing into that resistance.

Later, either we gave up,
or the force was switched off and our own motors took over,
bearing us to wherever we were bound.

Under that rocket-thrust, Cambridge fell back,
surfacing occasionally in our thoughts, our conversations,
our summaries of what had happened –
our Cambridge, unchanged, authentic, obsolete.

Wednesday
November 18, 1999
5 a.m.

SILENCE, WORSE

You inserted yourself into this life or that, mine for
    instance,
with care, paying attention to the surroundings,
trying not to disturb them, not to break anything.

You made a place for yourself and we accommodated you,
because you fended off your own magnitude with words –
and who wasn't won over by those words!

Now you've abandoned the place, though an effigy or
    after-image remains.
We try to engage it in conversation, but this smacks of
    idolatry.
Or we share memories of you and sometimes rather
    guiltily indulge in a little speculation.

It's not so much that we are trying to keep you alive,
as that we want to find out how death enters the picture.
We have to efface ourselves along with you, it hurts!

And as well as a sense of loss,
there's a sense of futility about all this –
only that, for the time being, silence seems still worse.

That silence seems worse is the poet's besetting sin.
What he speaks of, as often as not, is simply unsayable.
What he manages to say is all lies, or he couldn't say it.

Wednesday
November 18, 1999
Morning still

ALEXANDRA HOUSE

. . . Alexandra House was the place to be seen in
['Fidelity'', *Birthday Letters*]

It was like a measureless cavern, a temple,
with an altar in the centre, the Gaggia machine,
or was this before such contraptions? –
certainly, as you noted, it was before coffee-bars.

I experience again the excitement and the horror.
But the ambulant silhouettes are monochrome blanks.
I see bare floorboards and myself coming across them,
all eyes or none on me . . .

A whole world is stirring, with music, talk.
And beyond that, Cambridge itself,
and England. And beyond that,
the narrow seas and Europe. And

beyond that, the ocean and . . .
America, as it turned out –
for both of us.

NOT AUSTRALIA

You journeyed on. Not Australia.
America, instead. What did you discover there?
You wrote: "Crossing the continent destroyed something
　　in me."
And what was it you wrote about those small towns?

I too wrote of this, living in Coralville, Iowa.
"The sky's so blue, it dazzles.
Everything gleams, even the cobweb in the half-open
　　garage.
A few leaves tumble from delinquent trees . . ."

In 1975, on my fortieth birthday,
You wrote: "We're well past the age now when the Indian
　　princes handed over their affairs
and disappeared into the forest."

You extracted yourself, or were extracted,
and brought America back with you to low-intensity Great
　　Britain.
To this day the former shakes her head.
But no more did the latter understand, though crowning
　　you.

Meanwhile Australia's tattoo still rattled in your ears.
You'd stared in that direction, but your feet hadn't moved.

Monday
November 22, 1999
5 a.m.

BAIRNWICK

Stragglers line sections of the bookshelves;
living quarters have been quarried for a few female students,
whose things are draped over surfaces;
the depths, though, are undisturbed.

I try to imagine you here,
and a world emerges from behind the improvised later
    occupations.
We move through resistances.
When finally we leave, it's as if we had been ejected.

You're there still.
You're trying to deal with a situation.
You've had to come up with something
and are still not sure about it.
You are trying to make them out, your hosts.
You are about to retire, to take your uncertainties with you
    to bed,
to mull them over with Sylvia.

Bairnwick's closed on this as well.
Everything's ingeniously packed in there,
everything has its place,
and the door fits snugly.

You crossed this threshold all those years ago.

Saturday
November 27, 1999
Tennessee

LISTENING TO AN INTERVIEW WITH YOU,
TAPED IN COURT GREEN, AFTER
THE PUBLICATION OF *WOLFWATCHING*

I pay attention to the words,
as if they were not recorded words,
but you were speaking them at this moment,
and myself wanting to catch what you were saying just
    once,
explaining how you came to Yeats,
how you came to write *Shakespeare and the Goddess of
    Complete Being.*

I pay attention, as you'd have wished.
What you're saying is perfectly clear,
but then I've heard it many times.
Still, I can pretend I'm hearing it now for the first time
and getting it straight away,
pretend that the mind's working flawlessly,
that death has no business here.

Sunday
November 28, 1999
Tennessee

FLAGRANTE DELICTO

for S.H.

What a commotion!
What a flurry of activity!
Trying to manage it all, I suppose.
The *Oresteia, Metamorphoses, Alcestis, Sir Gawain* . . .

But the cancer was a big No!
A hand raised: Stop!
And there you were, with your swag,
in flagrante delicto!

The Gods were stirred up as well,
almost believing in themselves.
And you stood there, hands in pockets,
wondering, what next.

But that was one big No!

Thursday
December 2, 1999
5.30 a.m.

NOW

Now, listening to your voice
tells me that, though you are gone,
death's no greater.
Death's been reduced to a size, in fact,
as Brodsky said New York City reduced one to a size.
Death's been put in its place,
though that's cold comfort!

We can proceed,
as on a mild day with drizzle,
several ordeals behind us . . .

If the going of such as you can be appropriated by death,
then the world, too, is no greater.
Spirituality takes over.

But what of your words?
Well, they've detached themselves.
But they're not so much authorless,
as the author has released them
and is suspended alongside them.
They're coterminous with him, that is;
he may even be keeping an eye on them,
which is all he *can* do.

And what this may mean –
I've not yet tried, so cannot say for sure –
is I'll be able to read them
without being distracted by thoughts of their author,
which is you.

Which also means I'll maybe find them wanting?

That's a danger, but I'm alive to it –
and their undefensiveness is a kind of guarantee.

I'm trying hard to address you!
You're not listening.
Or you simply do not hear.
You're even walking away now.
I'll pay attention to your voice,
its settling in, its sagacity and patience.

Your appreciation of us is what comes to mind,
but now you're turning from us
to the work in hand, your work.

Sunday
December 5, 1999

Notes

Getting There (page 13)

I was in Iowa City, Iowa, when I learnt that Ted Hughes had died. My ex-wife Jill phoned with the news, in the early hours of October 29, 1998, having herself heard from Ted's sister Olwyn. Later, after I had let the family know that I would be coming over for the funeral, I again phoned Court Green, Ted's home in Devon. I spoke to Ted's daughter Frieda. There was some uncertainty about the arrangements.

Flowers (page 14)

The reference here is to our selection of English translations of Yehuda Amichai's poetry. I had several sessions with Ted in Court Green. We worked in the sitting-room, the room where the funeral bouquets and wreaths were collected.

Still (page 14)

fifty years ago Having "gone down" in 1954, Ted Hughes was nevertheless often to be seen in Cambridge shortly thereafter.

Intro (page 15)

the Great War Ted's imagination, of course, was partly formed by memories (through his father) of World War I.

my Uncle Joe's account of Auschwitz As a child, shortly after the end of World War II, I went to Paris with my mother and met my uncle Joseph, who (together with his younger brother Albert) had just returned from Auschwitz. He told us a little about the brutality and humiliation they had suffered.

Americas (page 16)

Over the Atlantic again As noted, I came to England for Ted's funeral (November 3rd, 1998). During this brief visit, I also went to Keele. I then returned to America, to Iowa City, and the University of Iowa. I had flown back and forth across the Atlantic about twice a year, for twenty-seven years.

Ally (page 17)

"a little uneasy" Some time in the Sixties, the editor of the Macmillan poetry series, Kevin Crossley-Holland, rejected a manuscript I had submitted on the recommendation of David Wevill. I think his courteously worded judgment was correct. Ted, however, disagreed and it did seem to me, in my more optimistic (if paranoid) moments, that everybody was deaf to my kind of music.

"Uncle Wolf" (page 18)

This designation of Ted was used by an American friend. Perhaps it is out of Native American mythology. Wolves concerned Ted (see, for instance, his poem "The Retired Colonel": "Here's his head mounted, though only in rhymes,/Beside the head of the last English/Wolf (those starved gloomy times! . . .") From his and Sylvia's flat in Chalcot Square, Primrose Hill, the wolves in nearby Regent's Park Zoo could be heard. In conversation with the Serbian poet, the late Vasko Popa, wolf stories were swapped, the wolf being the totem animal of the Serbs (see Popa's cycle "Wolf Salt", in *Collected Poems*, translated by Anne Pennington, introduced by Ted Hughes, 1978).

I did not visit It was suggested that I visit the wolves, in Regent's Park Zoo, when I came over for Ted's funeral in 1998.

"Dick, Jack, Dan,/And a curse on the age that loses the tune." See Ted Hughes's poem "Singers" (*Lupercal*, 1960).

Winter is Coming In (page 19)

I was thinking, perhaps rather jejunely, of the early English poem "Sumer Is Icumen In". I wanted to write a pure lyric at this point, not knowing how and hoping that it would, as it were, write itself if I invoked the old poem.

crows When we came out of St. Peter's Church, after the funeral service, it was raining and crows, as I thought, rose into the air cawing loudly. Actually, as I learnt later, they were mostly jackdaws, although there may have been a few crows among them!

Your Death? (page 20)

between Court Green and Exeter Ted would meet me at Exeter St. David's Station. We had many conversations travelling between his home and the station or vice versa. The sheer scale of him, in the confined space of his car, was sometimes overwhelming.

Silently (page 20)

János Pilinszky . . ."as if I had remained silent" The Hungarian János Pilinszky (1921–1981) is one of the East European poets we took note of in the 1960s, when we began the magazine *Modern Poetry in Translation*. In collaboration with another Hungarian poet and contemporary of Pilinszky, János Csokits, Ted translated a selection of the former's poetry (*Selected Poems*, 1976; new edition with some additional material entitled *The Desert of Love*, 1989). Ted Hughes's Introduction to this collection (reprinted in *Winter Pollen*) is among his most striking pieces. Addressing the question of post-Holocaust writing, he quotes Pilinszky: "I would like to write, as if I had remained silent."

Our Magazine (page 21)

Kim's flat I have written elsewhere about the early days of *Modern Poetry in Translation*. Here I am recalling the moment when Ted first mentioned the idea to me.

"At least a novelty" From a rather snotty though, on balance, positive review of the first issue of the magazine, which appeared in *The Times Literary Supplement*. That is to say, I took it as positive at the time, although when I look at it now, I am not quite so sure!

Narrative (page 23)

Yehuda's re-telling in English   Ted Hughes co-translated with
Yehuda Amichai (they produced two volumes of the latter's
poetry: *Amen*, 1977 and *Time*, 1979). In his Introduction to
Amen, Ted insists that his principal concern as translator has
been to preserve "the tone and cadence of Amichai's own voice
speaking in English . . ." He concludes: "So as translations
these are extremely literal. But they are also more, they are
Yehuda Amichai's own English poems."

Remember Cambridge! (page 24)

Your rendering of Sir Patrick Spens   As mentioned, we used to
gather frequently in the Anchor pub where we sang songs,
settings of Scottish ballads or Irish rebel songs (e.g. "The
Wearing Of The Green"). Among Ted's favourite was an adap-
tation of Sir Patrick Spens ("The king sits in Dunferling toune
. . .").

As for our qualms about Sylvia   Sylvia Plath's arrival at
Cambridge was heralded in various student publications,
including the newspaper *Varsity*, which featured a picture of
her in a bathing costume. Her poems duly appeared here and
there and were ironized over, if not savaged, by our little group,
a review even appearing in the mimeographed weekly
Broadsheet, which at the time was edited by David Ross (future
editor of *Saint Botolph's Review*) and myself. However,
although Ted's association with Sylvia began a little after this,
he somehow never quite forgave us. I find his loyalty to her
memory moving, although his more hostile critics can be
counted on to interpret it differently.

The Complete Works (page 24)

Timon of Athens . . . Pericles   Ted would not have been without
a single one of Shakespeare's plays (I believe he chided Sylvia
on having read only a dozen or so). He showed me portions
of the Shakespeare book as he was writing it and insisted on
my reading it and letting him know what I thought. Of course,

I was flattered, but actually I think a strong ulterior motive was simply to persuade me to read more Shakespeare. There was much of the pedagogue in Ted.

No Alias (page 25)

reincarnations, as Brodsky called them   The Russian poet Joseph Brodsky used to refer ironically to his life in America, after his earlier life in the Soviet Union, as his "American incarnation".

Both Ted and Joseph encouraged me in my translation of the Russian poet Nikolay Zabolotsky (1903–58). Zabolotsky propounded a kind of materialistic theory of immortality, unending life, through successions of reincarnation or metamorphoses. In a late poem, titled "Immortality", Zabolotsky writes: "I died many times. O, how many dead bodies / have I raised from my own body!"

Gordian Knot (page 27)

Ted's more radical feminist critics sometimes accused him, to put it very mildly, of irresponsibility. I was attempting here to set this into some kind of perspective, the context, at least, of a man who refused to play or pretend to play God. Ted tried to live a fairly normal life in the most abnormal of circumstances. Though there is no justifying or excusing the treatment he received, it is partly to this that we perhaps owe such late masterworks as his versions of *Phèdre*, *The Oresteia* and *Alcestis*.

Mnemonics (page 29)

your approach to memory   With all his versatility and perseverance, Ted was also a great believer in the value of memorization (not only as a mental exercise or training) and often tried to instil this belief in others. His Introduction, "Memorizing Poems", to his anthology *By Heart: 101 Poems to Remember* describes a technique, based on the invention of narratives linking the disparate elements or words / objects in a list.

Ted enjoyed playing this game and persuading others to join in. The apparent shakiness of my own memory now suggests to me a failure of nerve, but I fondly remember Ted's persuading me to try, on one or two of our river walks. I don't think I performed very well but I did better than I'd expected. In short, I was rather pleased with myself, surprised at the effectiveness of the technique, which I'd not taken on trust from him, even though his argument was persuasive. The perennial pedagogue, Ted duly applauded my efforts.

compensated for the limits placed on talk This game seemed to me to be a substitute for something else that Ted wanted to say, to find a way of saying, also having to do with memory, of course. He experimented more and more with this towards the end of his life. *Birthday Letters* was his last experiment in this particular mode.

Art Confused (page 31)

to excoriate free verse It seems to me that, along with Graves's Muse- or White Goddess-worship, we also acceded to his formalism. Ted, I believe, was somewhat under the influence also of another highly self-conscious, technically adept stylist, the Tennesseean poet and critic John Crowe Ransom, to whom he had probably been introduced by another Tennesseean, our friend Lucas Myers.

first-person poetry In general, it seems to me, much of the poetry that we wrote as students avoided the personal or at least self-revelatory. This was more in response to Graves's notions of poetry than to those of Eliot with his "objective correlative" and modernist injunction against the direct expression of emotions.

It seems to me that Ted really almost from the start was free of the prejudices we had somehow acquired with respect to personal or confessional poetry, although in a letter to me from America, in 1959, he had hypothesized (*à propos* Robert Lowell, who was unknown to me at the time) that "Autobiography is the only subject matter really left to Americans. The only thing an American *really* has to himself, and *really* belongs to, is his family . . ."

The white Goddess's magisterial eye, rather than Eliot's kept us under perpetual judgment "By that evening window where / his accurate eye keeps Woburn Square / Under perpetual judgement so / That only the happy can come and go . . ." ("Verses for the 60th Birthday of Thomas Stearns Eliot" from *News of the World* by George Barker). My unreliable memory led to my substituting "magisterial" for "accurate".

your own prodigious talent was no advantage Perhaps he would not have gone so far as to have said that, but certainly he continued to search for the means of direct expression, from his early literal assault on the problem, inventing a language for *Orghast*, to the re-telling of Ovid and to *Birthday Letters*. Ted Hughes's translation of Seneca's *Oedipus* (1968), used a deliberately restricted vocabulary, similarly trying to circumvent the conventions or English stage acting, or to substitute for them a more elemental representation of the emotions. The "super-ugly" diction of *Crow* was linked to the same radical project. It seems to me now, as it seemed to me then, that Ted felt he had almost to circumvent his great talent.

Translation (page 32)

"X-ray vision" The Hungarian poet János Csokits, who collaborated with Ted Hughes on the translation of János Pilinszky's poetry (see note on "Silently", page 91), describes their collaboration in his commentary, "János Pilinszky's 'Desert of Love': A Note" (*Translating Poetry: The Double Labyrinth*, ed. Daniel Weissbort, 1989). He describes in some detail what Ted Hughes required of him: "He did not want smooth and polished renderings in what he called 'magazine English' [. . .]. I tried to keep the poetic idiom of Pilinszky in English without exaggerated respect for the host language, hoping to preserve both the peculiar Hungarian flavour and the poet's personal style. [. . .] By sticking to the original, the English text inevitably becomes odd, but this oddity seemed to appeal to the translator [. . .]." But he adds: "I am convinced that my approach would never have worked without the special faculty of Ted Hughes to feel the quality, style and characteristics of a poem

even in the crudest word-for-word translation. It is almost as if he could X-ray the literals and see the original poem in ghostly detail like a radiologist viewing the bones, muscles, veins and nerves of a live human body. [. . .] The effect is not that of a technical device; it has more to do with extra-sensory perception."

He goes on to characterize the versions that resulted: "Without the softening effect of the original metre and rhyme scheme the impact of some of these poems can be very painful; they sound harsher and Pilinszky's view of the world appears grimmer than in Hungarian. These X-ray versions, then, are evidently not for the reader in need of a verbal soporific or a musical therapy against life.

We get a strong sense of Hughes's ability to work with the rawest raw material. Indeed, that is what he wanted and needed. Of course, he also benefited from help (Csokits's commentary on Pilinszky's poems are exemplary) but he could not even begin before he had the sense of having seen through to the centre of the poem, to its inspiration, and it was only the annotated ad-verbum renderings that helped him achieve this.

Clutter (page 33)

you said you liked clutter Ted was quite insistent about this, once enjoining me not to throw *any* papers or documents away! He also urged me to keep at least fifty copies of every issue of *MPT*. (Needless to say, I didn't follow this advice.) As I was clearing my house in Iowa City and disposing of sackfuls of miscellaneous papers and documents, I was reminded uncomfortably of Ted's injunction. However, I could not deal with all the debris without also reducing its volume. It is true, though, that once it had been reduced, there seemed less and less reason not to reduce it still further.

Feng Shui (page 34)

I heard of this now fashionable practice through Ted, on a visit to Devon, some three or four years ago. He gave me a book on the subject and told me, in Rilkean terms: "It will change your life!" However, there was more than a hint of mockery or self-mockery in his words. What seemed good about Feng Shui was that it activated or validated one's own instinct for order, harmony, tranquillity. I fuss over my immediate surroundings, moving objects about until I feel they are in the right place.

I regret my tendency to anecdotalize experiences that deserved rather better of me. I suppose this poem was a belated attempt to make amends.

Hear (page 35)

Jorge Luis Borges visited Iowa City once Borges lectured to a packed auditorium, at the University of Iowa. He sat at a table, on stage, and spoke into a microphone that was defective: a blind man talking inaudibly. Finally, someone had the guts to climb up and tell Borges what was happening, and eventually the fault was put right.

I am reminded of an image in Pilinszky's poem "The Passion", as translated by Ted Hughes and János Csokits: "In a glass-caged silence".

Court Green After (page 36)

Carol Hughes invited me to Court Green during the spring of 1999, when I was back in England for the duration, before having to return to Iowa for my last teaching semester. Very little, I suppose, had been changed since Ted's death.

Dutch translator It occurs to me, as a translator myself, that there may be a good deal of material of this sort, i.e. letters by writers to their translators, responding to questions. They might be more inclined to answer their translators candidly than they would an interviewer. The Dutch translator in question was working on *Birthday Letters*.

And the photo, 1954, Pembroke College graduates This framed photograph hung on the wall of the bedroom where I slept. I had slept here before, during Ted's life, but had not paid much attention to it. Now I studied it carefully. Ted was immediately identifiable. With only a little more difficulty I identified his friend Terence McCaughey as well.

the dead-reckoning eye Ted was a fine marksman. He was, unless I am mistaken, a half-blue in archery. I never saw him draw a bow, but I do remember our taking pot shots at tin-cans on a fence. He told me that he had once hunted but no longer did, although he still enjoyed marksmanship. His extraordinarily steady, level gaze, rather intimidating in fact, reminded me of this prowess of his.

Pedagogue (page 38)

"A Bedtime Story – Where you can't walk take a leap" Ted wrote this in the copy of *Shakespeare and the Goddess of Complete Being* that he gave me. I had, at his invitation or request, read sections, in an earlier version. I also benefited, or failed to benefit from several impromptu lectures by him on the subject. By the time he gave me the published book it seemed to me he was exasperated with me – more likely, I was exasperated with myself – for not devoting myself more wholeheartedly to Shakespeare.

Ted liked a poem I wrote about Shakespeare, or rather about my inability to read Shakespeare, about simply being too much in awe of him. Probably he felt that here I was at least genuinely trying to come to terms with the Bard, to arrive at some sort of working arrangement, so to speak. Or at least I was expressing annoyance with *myself*, which was a step in the right direction.

A Dedication (page 39)

The Zabolotsky volume I am referring here to my translation from the Russian of the poetry of Nikolay Zabolotsky. Ted included three of my early translations in his and Seamus Heaney's anthology *The Rattle Bag* (1982). He was particularly fond of these, probably because they tended to be quite literal. I sent him the near complete manuscript, and he offered to write an introduction. Seamus Heaney also offered to write something. When I mentioned this to Ted, he said that in that case he needn't do it! Later on, in view of his illness, it was out of the question anyway.

I'd coupled your name with Brodsky's I dedicated the book to the memory of Ted Hughes *and* Joseph Brodsky. As noted, Ted had supported my labours from the start, and Joseph Brodsky, who greatly admired Zabolotsky, had done likewise, though he was far more critical of my versions. At Brodsky's invitation, I visited him in New York, just before Christmas 1995 – he died on January 28th, 1996 – to work a little on the Zabolotsky. He was surprisingly keen to do so, evidently feeling that my translations, after such a prolonged period of gestation, were, in fact, not irredeemable. During our working session he too offered to write an introduction. He also offered to recommend the book to Farrar Straus & Giroux, which he duly did (they duly rejected it). Joseph died before he was able to write an essay on Zabolotsky.

How uneasily these two names occupy the same page Ted Hughes and Joseph Brodsky respected one another, although they were somewhat blind to one another's poetry.

Some Thoughts on the Thought-Fox (page 40)

My wife-to-be Valentina Polukhina urged me to try to remember some poems. All that came to mind were fragments of poems I had once known in their entirety. Later I played a game with myself, imagining various mini-anthologies I could assemble, collections of poems which for one reason or another I had hitherto committed to memory or had found myself remembering. I was thinking of Ted's anthology *By Heart: 101 Poems to Remember* and his Introduction to that collection, included also as an Afterword to the large anthology, *The School Bag*, edited by him and Seamus Heaney (see note on "Mnemonics", page 93).

my own "thought-fox" poem The poem in question concerns a moth drawn to my lighted window at night, presumably in Queens' College. It was one of the three short poems I contributed to *Saint Botolph's Review*. Only a single issue of this famous and extremely rare journal was published, in 1956. The party to launch the journal often crops up in critical studies of Hughes and/or Plath, as it is on that occasion that the two met (see Ted's poem "St. Botolph's", in *Birthday Letters*).

so often commented on by you See, for instance, "The Burnt Fox" (in *Winter Pollen*). The fox had appeared at his door in a dream, at the end of his first two years at Cambridge (1951–1953), during which he read English. It came at night, after he had been trying to write his final weekly essay, before the exams. The fox's humanoid body was charred, as though it had been roasted in a fire. It laid its burned, bleeding human hand palm down on the page on which Ted had been writing his essay. "Stop this – you are destroying us", it said, leaving a bloody print on the paper.

the Netsuke image on the cover of Wolfwatching *Wolfwatching* was published in 1989. The image on the cover was from an 18th-century Netsuke. It depicts a wolf-like creature, with an upraised, bushy tale, its front limbs folded, its head turned slyly or humorously to one side. It might be stealing away on tiptoes, or feigning shyness, or it might be like Ted's Thought-Fox. In any case, although the book's general appearance did not appeal to Ted, the little wolf did.

Couldn't we have applauded The fact is that Ted tended to be optimistic, which made his anger at and disillusionment with the behaviour of his critics so poignant. I now find myself wondering whether his friends – perhaps I should just speak for myself – could not have supported him more.

Black Ice (page 43)

In the Midwest, there is a good deal of freezing rain, which coats the bare trees (quite beautifully) and renders walking or driving almost impossible. The film of ice is sometimes virtually invisible, hence the term "black ice".

A Bad Mistake (page 46)

This may be presumptuous of me, but surely *Birthday Letters* was a preparation, a necessary clearing of the ground? It dealt with material, of which, given his situation, Ted felt he had to make a *public* disclosure. It was not the culmination of his entire life's work even if, in a sense, it might be thought to represent a culmination of one aspect or phase of it.

Taking You with Me (page 47)

Vivekananda I believe Henry Miller mentions this in one of the Tropics books. The notion is an uncomfortable one for us word-spinners! Ted, it seems to me, accepted the suffering, understood the silence of such as János Pilinszky or Paul Celan. And, of course, Pilinszky himself was not, in fact, silent. Celan, it is true, in the end, silenced himself.

Your Voice Inside the Abbey (page 48)

A Service of Thanksgiving was held in Westminster Abbey, on Thursday 13 May 1999 at 11.00 am, in the presence of Prince Charles and the Queen Mother.

that song from Cymbeline Finally, though, there was Ted himself, with the Song from Cymbeline ("Fear no more the heat o' the sun"). While the poem was on the Order of Service, it was not specified that we would actually be hearing Ted's own voice, although I suppose this might have been inferred, since no reader was named. The Song is to be found, of course, in *A Choice Of Shakespeare's Verse* (1971) which also includes Ted's "Note" (in fact, a magisterial essay) on Shakespeare.

The Song from Cymbeline is also in *By Heart: 101 Poems to Remember*. It was from the recording Ted made of all the poems in this book that his reading was taken.

life itself wanting you to live "How Water Began to Play", in *Crow*, begins: "Water wanted to live"; the refrain is "it came weeping back". When I substituted "life itself" for "water",

I dare say I meant "we", those of us in the Abbey who knew and loved the man.

In Greys (page 50)

what did they make of you I imagine that for Vasko Popa, János Pilinszky, Zbigniew Herbert, Miroslav Holub, Ted was not just a well-intentioned writer from "over there", an ally in the Western literary world. Nor was he exactly a kindred spirit. He brought with him more than sympathy. It seems to me that he brought a vision of what they were, which, given his rootedness in the English tradition, in Shakespeare, was particularly valuable. Ted was the rarest of links between writers, being a writer of great stature himself, not simply a facilitator of cultural intertraffic.

I wrote this poem, as indicated, in the ancient spa town of Karlovy Vary (Carlsbad), Czech Republic, not so far from the late Miroslav Holub's home town of Plsen (Pilsen).

Eel-Fishing (page 52)

Ted quite often took me with him to visit Peter and Terry Norton-Smith, through whose property flowed a fine trout stream. We would tramp down to the river and, on this particular occasion, we (or rather, they) fished for eels. Ted had told me about the intricate life-cycle of eels, which start their immense journey in the Sargasso Sea, in the North Atlantic, finding their way back to the very same streams in England and elsewhere, year after year. He had dreamt up a scheme (unrealized, of course) for marketing eels, a great delicacy and no longer the proletarian dish of generations before.

as during the blitz Peter Norton-Smith was a highly decorated RAF bomber pilot during World War II. In other words, he belongs to that group of men who were my principal boyhood heroes.

You lent me a rod I think this was the only time in my life that I actually tried my hand at fishing. So great was my desire to acquit myself honourably that I succeeded in snapping a supposedly unbreakable rod, although presumably – this has been suggested to me since; it rather spoils the story! – there was some fault in it.

Letters from Iceland (page 53)

In summer 1999, Valentina and I went to Iceland for two weeks. We were given a rather pleasant university flat in Reykjavik with balcony and views across to the ocean. Our Icelandic friend took us on several expeditions into the interior of his astonishing country.

You'd have homed in on this land / Not like Auden & MacNeice I'd not read *Letters from Iceland*, so I bought the book and read it there, finding it entertaining but also disappointing, almost sophomoric. I contrasted the authors' account with what I imagined Ted might have managed had he written about the country. He was, in fact, very interested in Norse legends and was trying to compose an appreciation of *The Complete Sagas of Icelanders* (1997), which was in his library (presumably he had agreed to write a blurb and, due to his illness, had found it hard going).

"a gigantic cinder" In a letter to me. Most visitors are struck by Iceland's power, literal power in terms of thermal energy.

Geyser's little brother greeted us My friend, Astradur Eysteinsson, remembers the incident: "Geyser, the old 'original' geyser itself, no longer erupts unless powerfully provoked (with masses of soap, basically). But his little brother, or son, Strokkur, erupts regularly every ten to fifteen minutes. However, when we approached him again, on the way back from Gullfoss, he erupted twice in quick succession, clearly giving you and Valentina a double sign from the heart."

I think we shared some such dream There was an uncluttered feel to Reykjavik. Conditions there felt to me almost ideal for work. I imagine Ted as agreeing.

Cornucopia (page 55)

Last night, in Devon A tranquil, delicious and well lubricated dinner remembering Ted is the backdrop to this piece.

that photograph / of you with my small son Benjamin I recently found this photograph of Ted and my son Benjamin, taken at a wedding tea at the Savoy Hotel. My memory of the picture had not been accurate but the scene as depicted here is correct. Ben, his head cocked, is looking up, not as I remembered it at Ted, but at the camera. Ted is, indeed, smiling rather goofily and is looking down at his plate, delighted, as if mesmerized by the food.

Not Saint Botolph's: an Antidote (page 58)

A kind of antidote It pleases me, of course, to think that *MPT* may have played a part in helping Ted to start writing again.

Betrayal? (page 59)

"A Kurdish practice" During my last semester in Iowa I suffered from a painful hip – it turned out to have been the early stages of arthritis. I went to a massage person who tried various techniques, including the Kurdish one described here.

On Your Retinue (page 61)

You'd this retinue I think of Ted as a "king player". He enjoyed eating out, banqueting with friends and visitors. In the babble of these soirées, Ted himself was an extraordinarily central and solid figure, a fatherly presence, at the same time expansive, even extravagant. The scale of the man impressed itself at such moments in a manner that may well be described as kingly.

dragging them behind I had in mind "Sonnet Partly of Rats" by Daniel Huws, first published in *Saint Botolph's Review*: "Dragging six hundred dead and swollen rats at my heels". This association of mine is not very flattering to us, the retinue!

Venice and the Rice Diet (page 62)

I announced I was going to Venice   Never having been to Venice
before, I was quite excited at the prospect. (I went with
Valentina, mainly to visit Joseph Brodsky's grave.) Presumably
Ted hadn't been there either. The chances of his ever seeing
Venice were now remote, but that thought did not occur to me
at the time.

the diet of rice   is as described here. In my refusal, I suppose,
to recognize the seriousness of Ted's illness, I was surprised at
his less than enthusiastic response. I am now shocked at my
own obtuseness.

A Translation (page 63)

What is intriguing about this, of course, is that he felt able to
rewrite the English version, without reference to any source
text.

   It is interesting that he is able, in this situation, simply to
write his own version, based on someone else's, whereas in
other circumstances, i.e. when faced by the poet himself or by
the source text in a literal translation, he feels compelled to stay
as close as possible to the wording and even syntax of the orig-
inal.

Lucky! (page 65)

Sean and his wife   Sean was the Scottish poet, the late Sean
Rafferty, who lived in total obscurity, not far from Ted's home.
Ted regularly visited him bearing gifts, taking me along on
several such occasions.

Saint Botolph's Review (page 66)

that red-nosed piano player   I attended the party, on Ted's
urging, in spite of a bad cold. At the time, I used to try to play
jazz piano. On this occasion, I blearily supplied a vamping piano
accompaniment to another friend, since deceased, Joe Lyde.
Joe played the trumpet quite professionally.

"planetary certainty" See Ted's self-castigatory poem "St. Botolph's" in *Birthday Letters*: "I had predicted / Disastrous expense, a planetary / Certainty, according to Prospero's book. / Jupiter and the full moon conjunct / Opposed Venus [. . .]."

Hartland (page 70)

Hartland Point is a beauty spot in North Devon, on the western extremity of Bideford Bay. Great cliffs afford a view over to the island of Lundy.

Was it Nature? (page 74)

your otter "An Otter", *Lupercal*: "Re-enters the water by melting."

A Hypothesis (page 75)

Was it that the prose did you in Once, when I announced that I was writing something in prose, Ted warned me against it. On the other hand, his approval of one's attempts to write poetry was always quite tangible. Although he wrote some wonderful prose himself – essays, reviews, stories, tales for children, the Shakespeare book finally – I recall his uneasiness about it.

as your Thought-Fox had warned? See notes on "Some Thoughts on The Thought-Fox", pages 99–100.

Translation's muse beckoned While translation was, perhaps, a saving grace for Ted in the early '60s, it became at the end of his life a hard taskmaster. Of course, his work with Aeschylus, Euripides, Ovid helped him towards a goal, but at the same it was enormously, even catastrophically, demanding. Ted could never give less than everything. I ask, then, as a translator myself: Was it translation, more specifically than prose, that did the damage? Did he not need an extra life to accomplish what he set out to do?

Our *Cambridge* (page 76)

I steal the title of this poem from a book, *Our Cambridge* (1977).

only to malign or mock it While we were all bright fellows and some of us had come to Cambridge on Scholarships or Exhibitions, we did not fit in, or we refused to. Nevertheless, we had "arrived".

the alternative Cambridge we cobbled together We, that is the Botolph's group, adopted a sometimes confrontational attitude towards what we regarded as the establishment (the term "establishment" was not yet current). We imagined we were making quite an impact on Cambridge, but I rather fancy we were not.

Alexandra House (page 79)

For an accurate description of this establishment, also known as the Soup Kitchen, see Ted Hughes's poem "Fidelity", in *Birthday Letters*: " . . . Gutted, restyled/À la mode, the Alexandra House/Became a soup-kitchen. Those were the days/Before the avant-garde of coffee bars./The canteen clatter of the British Restaurant,/One of the war's utility leftovers,/Was still the place to repair the nights with breakfasts./But Alexandra House was the place to be seen in."

My own memory of the place is far less precise. Also, the episodes I associate with Alexandra House, at least those that involved myself, are of a less adult nature than that which Ted describes so beautifully. Still, the Soup Kitchen remains in my memory, like a tune associated with some long gone lover.

Not Australia (page 80)

At about the time I met Ted, just before Sylvia appeared on the scene, he was planning to emigrate to Australia, to join his older brother Gerald. He did visit Australia later, although we never discussed this. The point is that when I met him he was on the point of leaving England, probably for good. Instead, he went to America with Sylvia. America was the dream country, his (I suspect) as well as mine. Although this was something we may have had in common, we never really discussed it either. He wrote me two or three letters from his America and, much later, I wrote many letters to him from mine, and he answered some of these. Even at the time, I thought that he was holding back, not conveying, as he had begun to do in those very early letters, his somewhat darker vision of the country. Only when I wrote to him in 1982, telling him I had cancer, did he write quite emphatically, urging me to return to England, live off welfare (sic!) and devote myself fully to writing, enthroning myself, telling the world to fuck off etc. That he was speaking from the heart, indeed with considerable passion, was quite evident. Of course, I chose a different path. Ted would never directly warn or counsel, because he did not want to confuse one, but he hinted as broadly as he dared! Only now, re-reading those letters, do I hear what he was saying.

Meanwhile, Australia's tattoo still rattled in your ears My conjecture, of course. Ted was, in fact, at least as interested in Native American as in Aboriginal folklore.

Bairnwick (page 81)

"Bairnwick" is the name of the former residence of the Myers family, on the campus of the University of the South, Sewanee, Tennessee. The house was gifted to the University by the Myers children, after the death of their parents. Ted and Sylvia came here and stayed for a while, although Lucas himself, their friend, was not in Sewanee at the time. I never met the Myers parents, but Ted did and I remember his talking about them.

Lucas's father had been Professor of Religion at the University. Lucas took me on a tour of the campus, although it was pretty thoroughly misted in. On two occasions, we visited the house, now a dormitory for a few female students. There was still a residue of the Myers library on the shelves.

Listening to an Interview with You, Taped in Court Green, after the Publication of Wolfwatching (page 82)

While I was staying with Lucas and Dawa Myers, we listened to a tape of this quite excellent interview with Ted.

Now (page 84)

reduces one to a size In a documentary film about him, Joseph Brodsky, who lived and died in New York, comments on the giant city's tendency to "reduce you to a size". I suppose it was the way he put it, in particular his non-standard use of the indefinite pronoun, that made this notion somehow memorable.

Death, of course, reduces man to a size, but here I found myself reversing this, death – in particular Ted's – being itself reduced to a size. Perhaps I was helped towards this by Ted's own concentration on death or Death in his poems, his interest, for instance, in the Tibetan Book of the Dead, the *Bardo Thodol*.

You're not listening Obviously this whole piece is about listening. When I listen to recordings of Ted's voice now, I have to take into account what to me is still incomprehensible, his disappearance. There is so much that he himself has set going, that his own absence from the scene is somehow unimaginable, even though it is a fact. Reading Ted's words now, I find that although I can understand better what they are conveying, I am reluctant for this to happen if it means allowing him, as it were, to be dead, no longer an active part of the process of reception. I see him as still formulating what he has to say. The words are provisional and I resist their becoming more definitive. So, at the end of this poem, I imagine Ted returning to his proper business, to "the work in hand".

Some new and recent poetry from Anvil

GAVIN BANTOCK
Just Think of It

OLIVER BERNARD
Verse &c.

NINA BOGIN
The Winter Orchards

PETER DALE
Under the Breath

DICK DAVIS
Belonging

HARRY GUEST
A Puzzling Harvest
COLLECTED POEMS 1955–2000

MICHAEL HAMBURGER
From a Diary of Non-Events

PHILIP HOLMES
Lighting the Steps

GABRIEL LEVIN
Ostraca

E A MARKHAM
A Rough Climate

DENNIS O'DRISCOLL
Exemplary Damages

SALLY PURCELL
Collected Poems

GRETA STODDART
At Home in the Dark

JULIAN TURNER
Crossing the Outskirts

Some poetry in translation from Anvil

DANTE: *The Divine Comedy*
Translated by Peter Dale

NIKOS GATSOS: *Amorgos*
Translated by Sally Purcell

GOETHE: *Roman Elegies* and other poems
Translated by Michael Hamburger

LUIS DE GÓNGORA: *Selected Shorter Poems*
Translated by Michael Smith

NIKOLAY GUMILYOV: *The Pillar of Fire*
Translated by Richard McKane

YEHUDA HALEVI: *Poems from the Diwan*
Translated by Gabriel Levin

NÂZIM HİKMET: *Beyond the Walls*
Translated by Ruth Christie and Richard McKane

POEMS OF JULES LAFORGUE
POEMS OF FRANÇOIS VILLON
Translated by Peter Dale

IVAN V. LALIĆ: *Fading Contact*
Translated by Francis R Jones

FEDERICO GARCÍA LORCA: *A Season in Granada*
Edited and translated by Christopher Maurer

PO CHÜ-I: *The Selected Poems of Po Chü-i*
Translated by David Hinton

VASKO POPA: *Collected Poems*
Translated by Anne Pennington and Francis R Jones

RAINER MARIA RILKE: *Turning-Point*
Translated by Michael Hamburger

RABINDRANATH TAGORE: *Song Offerings*
(Gitanjali)
Translated by Joe Winter